AF251810

KILLING TIME

Seymour Mayne

MOSAIC PRESS
OAKVILLE–LONDON

Copyright © 1992 by Seymour Mayne.

Book design by Mary Vindicé.

Cover drawing by Sharon Katz,
after Rembrandt: *Abraham's Sacrifice*.

No part of this book may be reproduced or transmitted
by any means, electronic or mechanical, including
photocopying and recording information storage
and retrieval systems, without permission in writing
from the publisher, except by a reviewer who may
quote brief passages in a review.

Published by MOSAIC PRESS, P.O. Box 1032, Oakville, Ontario,
L6J 5E9. Offices and warehouse at 1252 Speers Road,
Units 1 and 2, Oakville, Ontario, L6L 5N9 Canada.

Mosaic Press acknowledges the assistance of the Canada Council
and the Ontario Arts Council in support of its publishing programme.

Printed and bound in Canada.

Cataloguing in Publication Data

Mayne, Seymour, 1944 –
Killing Time

ISBN 0-88962-494-1

I. Title.
PS8576.A88K5 1992   C811'.54   C91-094339-7
PR9199.3.M38K5 1992

CONTENTS

I

DOWN HERE

You went up and we almost forgot you.
We got busy down here collecting
and sorting the coins and reluctant rings.
Up went the molten fire like our hearts
ready to sing towards the wide Sinai sky.

The women did not give in, refused us
their trinkets and called us headstrong fools.

But we celebrated and feasted
and settled down to a new routine.
A little bowing and praying here,
the priests egging us on there—so passed
the tranquil weeks of your absence.

And now you have come down among us.
Anger devours you and you spit
insults, curses and dire warnings.
We needed something to hold aloft
against the desert night.

Would that we had heeded our women,
more sagacious than Aaron's smug brood!

From His merciless retribution
and your unyielding wrath spare us now—
your murderous avengers,
the sons of Levi,
today have spilt enough of our blood.

Yes, we've heard much about him
now that he has settled down south.
One day here he brought three guests
home with him—somehow they suddenly
appeared, he said. Oh yes, I know
he still gathers people to himself.
Look at his retainers, I am told,
at the fields overrun with his sheep
and the loyal shepherds who followed him
and performed upon themselves
the bloody rite.
                    Me he abandoned
with our father. Stormed out,
left behind our idols and the broken
limbs of the gods he shattered.
About his own brother, the keeper
of clay, he is silent. He never
speaks of me, they tell me, never
so much as mentions my name.

He's been to Egypt; almost got
himself into dreadful trouble there
with my beautiful sister-in-law,
his wife, that is. And then
that awful business with the handmaiden.
If he could turn his back on us,
he could throw out a son. And now
the second has been born, an old merchant
bore the news to us. Let him prosper
and have many more. Who knows,
our sons may yet meet in the future?
But with our different gods
it can never be good, I fear.

Never. We'll always be strangers
and my sons and their sons, how
will they speak of him—
him, whom the others revere—
who long ago stopped
acting like a brother?

Reaching towards the fire
he wanted to save
the crying animals
breathing their last
but sentinels with flaming weapons
stood at the entrance
sheathed in withering light.

"Merkor and Shamlock,
hold your own," he shouted.
But the furred beast frightened
retreated towards the tongue
of fire, and the small predator
who always shaped a grin
with his whiskers, shrank
close by his larger mate.

Nothing availed them.
He strode forward, flames
waving towards his head.
He crouched, fell over, lay
prostrate, then crawled
over the threshold, rose—the air
was acrid with sacrifice
and his eyes smarted from smoke.

Cut in two as if to join
together again, on both sides
bodies wholly burnt
lay rigid and silent.
No tears came.
He stood there
stammering.

Someone grabbed his elbow,
someone else the right, and he
let himself be led through
the gauntlet of ash—his lips
praying upon the silence.
And then suddenly when he awoke
wondered why the bedclothes stank
and the roar of morning made him cry.

The rainbow we were supposed
to behold the next day
or the day after
never appeared.
Our eyes grew strained,
our necks stiff,
and the heavy ashen clouds
settled over the hills and streams.
The fish rose to the top
and rolled over
like silver bombers in maneuvers.

Who could believe it?
No rainbow, no
break of colour, no
sign? Someone's forgotten,
we reasoned.
And we began to pray
for the cleansing rains again
and the waves rising
to wash our cities—
friend's and foe's alike—
with the green tow of return.

V   LAST CHANCE

He ushered them all in hurriedly
and wondered—had he done right?
Why was he obeying the loud commands
given in the dead of darkness?
Why not abandon everyone
to shriek and howl
as the waves begin to rise
and water rushes in
to flush out mole, weasel and worm?
Let everything drown.
There will be no other time
or need to bring down
the doom of wrath.
Whoever broke this upon us,
let Him also stare
into the abyss of despair—
this is His last chance.

VI ADAM

If he had not smelled it, he would
never have known: the morning, sulphurous,
rose before his eyes like smoke.

Later, the afternoon assailed
his ears: the lancing glare of the sun,
open, loud, offering no respite.

Was this where he belonged?

Nighttime he groped his way
and found her beside the sentinel trees.
Heard her greeting, went up to touch,
her scent in his nostrils:
in anticipation he could taste
the lips that filled his eyes.

At dawn he prayed
the sulphur would
burn away in the rising light.

It was the day a little dust
first blew up by the healthy foliage;
then another gust, and slowly
shaping into form, the creature
finally sat there staring
wide-eyed at the light, absently
at the profusion of plants
and crying animals.

And that was the last day
everything was good.

II

EVEN WORDS

They don't do it anymore,
the sleepwalkers.
Now the extinct
bothersome bipeds
stalk their dreams and eat
everything in sight,
even words.

They put you down like that,
thinking you'd be comfortable for ages.
No one believed the hint of a smile
that snaked into your death mask.
You must have lain there waiting
for the top to snap shut
so you could turn over finally,
and when no one was looking,
sleep on your belly like a babe,
your last words gagging in your mouth
that stuttered like a rattle.

It is—has no other edges. Walk into the humid light; everything aspires to evergreen. And what is left forgets about icicles and wind, lives a moment, sprouts noises that cry out for the hegemony of words.

After brushing your teeth for sleep
you rise three times
like the man in the blemished legend:
First, to break the toothpick
into nine lucky pieces;
then to reach for the nighttime book;
And finally to spread some lip balm
over your lips so that the words
will not catch and bruise
on the dry and scaly patches.

V   TRACE

It is not a known
woman who sits before me.
Nor my unborn daughter.

Stranger than the masks
of the ancients,
you, face, stare
while around you the burning
landscape flares into flame,
caravans flee in every direction
seeking refuge.

Yet the trace of your word
is there upon my head—
soft touch of its weight,
how it cups the space
like a canopy.

i

Still air
   and its light sadness.
Day of snow—
   the street silent.
Few boots sunk
   into the feathery fall.

As I carry
   the shape of your face,
someone will take on
   the burden of our eyes.

ii

That silence of cold,
   even the winds die down—
   streets freeze
   in their ruts.

I am afraid
   no one will bolt
   this noiseless hour
   and we will all give in.

iii

Lifting the light snow
    we throw it over,
    spoil the clean sheen
    of a dune—
Then sunder
    the razor ridge
    the wind has perfectly
    honed.
That has its satisfaction.
    To get round the wind,
    outwit it.

for Liba and David Augenfeld

With a daughter
in the house,
will we be spared
the voice
and its awful command?

And the long
trip up mountainslopes,
the terrible
preparations, the heart
stabbed suddenly with fear

as the knife
glinting in the sun
takes on the ironic
smile of a guardian
angel;

and the foolish ram
caught there in the bushes
and my child's voice:
Who was it that spoke,
father? Was it you
all along?

III

SENTINEL SISTERS

How many
safe minutes left
to that moonless
midnight?

That is all
the time
we may get
and then

who will
speak
of the light
or darkness?

for Shoshi Hyman

i

This is not the day to write, but the worm shows
itself as a faint echo inching its way into the voice.
It grows fat, this stubby maggot of envy; it grows
and moves its way like a slug across the page.

Pour salt upon its tail. Sprinkle stinging caustic
upon its head and it will bloat and explode.

ii

The wind knows no destruction as yet. The sun
holds back the withering fire. We pray silently; the
leaves turn towards the sky and then populate the
night, dew upon their edges.

Tomorrow, far off in the distant north, the crazed
captains will resume the frightful carnage.

iii

You have all fled. There is no one on the high
ridges; no one even hiding among the prickly
bushes. No one waiting in the expectant silence of
the noon hour.

You have taken the faces of the aged and you
remember nothing that your bodies once knew. Food
and drink you bless trembling; no one leaps beyond
their words. And no one—as yet—bends an ear to
the still dim but rising echo of weeping.

iv

Once it was autumn rain that sealed the prayers
and the days of this season. Now there is no need to
measure our words. The sun, sand and silence are
sentinel sisters to festive devotion and meditation.

v

The great festival, begun in joy and contemplation—
if only we could undo most of our acts. Call back the
spiteful words, and banish the small mean-minded
predators of jealousy—

But we can't. For now we barely hold them in check.

vi

Too wilful. But who will coax the words to come?
Perhaps there is no need for speech. Sitting or standing
in the sun or shade, sink into speechlessness.

vii

He stalks everywhere here.
That is why there are so many children.

Let them all shriek, frolic.
Those cries keep strangers away.

And if they stay put where they are,
we can forget the vigil for a moment—

Just for a moment, she said to her sisters.

viii

Hold his hand
though he cannot speak.
Place your fragrant
fingers in his mouth.
His tongue retracts
from your touch,
a blind creature
inching out of the seaside
cave, slowly
on the long road
to amphibian being.

Do you hear? Or have your ears been stopped up with the welter of too many cries?

They sway and intone David's words of praise— the ancient shepherd's, the chants of nameless warriors fallen for Judea—the women beseeching you for life, the women at your silent tomb who line up here in the night and fill the surrounding field.

Listen, mother, listen to their cries, you whose breath left you as Benjamin was torn from your side—spare the barren so your cry never dies in agony but springs forth renewed on the lips of the newly born.

Heshvan 5748

IV   FROM MOUNT SCOPUS

for Sidra Ezrahi

Is it or is it not
a city, towers
on the heights,
the sky falling back
all around as if
the earth were rising?

Billowing
in the Judean
wind, your skirt.
You give
your smile
to the sun
and let the lines
of your face
run wild
in the brief riot
of your solitude.

Only the words
stay behind
teasing the mind
intimidated
by citadel and stone
that teach
flesh
the despair
of imitating them.

for Shlomo Vinner

The silence on the heights—nothing is heard from the neighbouring hill. The cries must be wandering in the valleys. The lost tribes of vows have disappeared among us and once in a while we recognize them—for a moment—in our chameleon speech.

The neighbour, Mr. Levy,
just doesn't stop
watering his cobbled walk.
Morning, afternoon, evening
he hoses it down.
The pinkish stones,
wet and glistening,
rarely get time to dry.
Why does he drench
them every day
washing them so often?

His words
nor his gestures
give it away,
but I suppose
watering the stones
keeps him from dozing,
and dozing
is the lazy sister
he wishes to avoid
in his retired years.

Besides, what's wet
is alive. Dust
can not return
to dust
when it's flowing—
or sticky
like vital mud.

Jerusalem

You can't talk
to Levy, that's for certain,
and you don't need
the good neighbours
to convince you.
He flies off the handle
at the least little word.
Ask him politely
to take a two day recess
from washing his walk
and he'll begin
to squawk,
then his voice rises
and he sputters forth
like an old red hose
loose at the top
and yells how
he never washes it daily
though it's plain
to hear and see
he can't get it
clean enough and must
flood it incessantly.

There's no
answering him then
so caught up
is he in his defense
you back off
and pity
the poor pink stones
still damp
and weepy
from the most recent abuse.

Jerusalem

VIII AT NIGHT THE DEW

for Don Stephens

At night the dew
    shines like the patina
        on an eye

and everything tall,
    standing rooted,
        begins to dart from sight—

I flee with the trees, fronds,
    birds and flying mites
        and take shelter

resting upon the stone
    that sweats lightly—

my forehead filled
        with dreams of rungs

rising into blinding light.

Mornings annihilate. The sun rises
steady like an executioner whose own
day will come. There is no redeeming us
under the unending skies. We flap
against each other, squawk, tear
away a limb, a foolish tongue
and nothing stays the consuming fire.

IV

KILLING TIME

KILLING TIME

I

From the towers
    and domed roofs
the voices leap—

but who needs
    God's help
if he or she speaks

wrestling with the adept
    figure of silence?

At midnight, a long whistle—bird or burglar's signal? Without warning, words dent the stillness: a man making a racket calls out for his dog.

In the morning, no trace of voice or bark. Did they grow suddenly—fast shoots breaking up through the dark—to die in the early silence?

*   *   *

Small chattering birds
    on the lilac twigs—
late afternoon
    bloom of light.

What season is it?

All that is temporary
    persists;
the holiday is brief
    but returns
again next year
    in Jerusalem.

III

As much as we can sleep, we take as a shield against the clamorous day.

The dead do not hear how each word of theirs makes claims upon us.

Who can completely free themselves of death's double mortgage?

IV

We will never meet him for long upon the worn cobbled stones. A wraith—his garments slipping—he reappears just for a moment, startles the keepers of the keys, the guardians and priests, yet disappears before the crowds can gather to chant his name or the prayer for the perfect day.

But his thin body enflames the young. They go in search of quarry and call upon him as they profane their hands with neighbour's blood.

Look, he won't come
     back; he's no fool.
Once he got wind
     of what's going on,
he found a brave way
     to hightail it
out of here.
     Sure, he opened
his big mouth,
     said too much,
got into real hot
     water—but
what did he expect,
     the damn fool,
that they'd crown
     him king and forever?

They pinned him
     down and then
those foolish followers
     of his began
to scurry around
     announcing
visions, miracles—
     and who among
the ignorant mercenaries
     could contradict them?
They left behind enough
     stories to confuse
the credulous.

They wanted to see
    him bless
the unleavened bread,
    the wine,
and tell the tale
    of flight
once again, down
    into the long
festive night, if only
    there was to be
enough time.
             Stretch
    it out,
stretch the hours—
    the festival
will protect us
    from the burly
recruits, the festivities
    will keep
everyone busy
    celebrating—

Who has the stomach
    to break a man,
his arms, legs, or spirit
    at this time?

*   *   *

And then the bleat
      of young sheep,
blood on the lintels
      of Egypt,
and the angel
      carrying out
the call
      of vengeance—

Memory feeds
      flesh
and a freed people.

Seven nights, seven
    days—
the lean and large
    cattle, Joseph's
alphabet of dreams;
    and the sevenfold years
gathering to a jubilee.
Give a portion
    to the needy;
stand up for
    the broken
in spirit and body;
    do not permit
the old to slip
    into the infirmity
of bitterness.

What is it that undermines—the centuries of wandering, constant flight, the new reins of power that we hold too tightly lest the powerlessness return and we are thrown again into bloodsoaked ditches?

And the desert soil took them for final sleep; and here we live with the nightmare they take to their graves.

We spring up in their death dreams; all the living run, scurry and hide—but we know it is the dead who dream us into being, their words put into our mouths for life.

If we do not tell
     the story
in haste
     as we flee
it unfolds
     us—
one way,
     the other way
we wander
     to the climax
of Sinai
     and then try
to turn away
     for it is always
high above, out
     of sight.

Give us a
    sign,
the part
    particle
of a word,
    the telltale
breath between
    consonants,
the sworn
    vowels
like ancient
    matriarchs
calling all
    their children
home to each
    other's
arms, praying
    they are
spared
    erasure's
unfeeling harm.

The song of Moses
    when he beheld

the Egyptians
    drowning;

the singing
    when he beheld . . .

when he beheld
    the song . . .

the singing
    after the seeing,

the singing
    blocking out—

the tongue no
    longer knows

what the eyes
    may have seen.

There is a fear there in the north; but it is not of leviathans or the space that swallows even silence in its vast dumbness. It is the fear of the heart, its need to pulse into speech and find a tongue to bring children into the resonant circle of chronicle and story.

The face does not falter; speech is held back as if it were dammed up to burst out later—but it never does in the north. The iceberg tongue hides a deeper shadow, the heart frozen right down to the depths, to the roots of words.

The hours,
    the numerology
of days,
    gematria
of breath—
    seek
out the hidden
    combination,
subtract
    add,
multiply
    or divide—
something always
    gives,
and we pray
    we do not have
to yield
    much more
to the measureless
    darkness.

The morning
        comes too soon,

banishes even
        the lingering

nightmare that
        darkness

will abide
        and even fire

itself will
        cease

to break out
        into light.

XVII

They can never
   stop

mending walls,
   pointing brick.

Nothing is maintenance
   free,

not even words.

The low mountains—
    worn

down by snow
    and massive ice.

Whatever we
    dream

is empty of
    face now,

of voice. Even
    upon the stone

escarpments we have
    given

up counting or
    killing time.

V

THE ORANGES OF SICILY

The oranges of Sicily
    yield sanguine red
but does anyone in Bologna
    take notice or mind
as the juice, squeezed
    into glasses
straight as the towers,
mixes with water amnesic
    as the young?

The tongue vows
    it is sweet,
the eyes beg pardon,
arms do not resist
    as fingers
tear away the fragrant
    skin,
and the aroma tells
    no one
the fruit drawing from
    underground sources
punish the flagrant wanderer
    who partakes
of the refreshing flesh
    but can not wholly
forget his brother's blood.

Bologna
May 1988

I thought my father's
name was Adam

but the scar above my eyes—
Cain's, they said, Cain's,

and smiled like crones
or little children just

learning how to speak,
how to wield words.

What is he up to again,
packing up just like that and taking
   my boy with him?
Tightlipped and stubborn—
I suppose that is what gave him strength
   to leave the casting of idols,
to push us on as we wandered
   south towards new strangers.
But this time there is a glint
   of a deeper darkness in his eyes
and I shudder helping the women flatten
   out the wheat cakes.
The ways of men bring trouble.
I pray, I heed the rules, but I will not laugh
   until he is returned to me.
Isaac, precious one, listen to him
   and be good,
I instructed while biting down sharper
   words for his obstinate father.
Going on a trip at this time of the year
   and at his age?
My little one, why did he pack the animal
   with kindling and sticks?
He should have carried you and had you pulled
   from his loins!
Instead he dreams to himself and announces
   he must obey
the commands given only to him in the late
   night silence
when on the hilltop he leans on that crook
and allows no one near him, human or beast.

Set the fire below your own head,
stick the blade's point in your own throat,
Moloch!

for Enrico Bellio

Sent forward,
our children
—we surmise—

may yet take
that enemy
by surprise.

   SOUND SONNET

for Larry Eldredge

There is altogether too much noise,
you will not dispute, and if you do,
it will only add to the general din.
Children can not forget their crying;
mothers, the cries that accompany birth—
fathers trying to smother them in their chests
guiltily hug their daughters, living
form of their most voluble moods.
There is altogether far too much noise.
Stifle it. A pen can do wonders; siphons
off torrents of the tongue and throat
and lets them all die into the contortions
of script. Immutable letters
stand where our voices have fallen.

Painfully the amphibious angels are dragging
        themselves
up from the sea—their wings eroded, rotting,
and eyes closing with a heavy darkness.
No sport now nor antics. The shore
is a sewer of dying flesh and God's
nose has begun to smart again.

He could not believe she was anything
but alive, all breath
and he would enter on the wing
of a long gasp and take the wind
in stride with her.

But he looked away
no longer than a moment.
A glimmer gave hope a second chance.
Later waking, he found brittle ash;
she was not there beside him. Perished—
but he could not admit it.

Somewhere nearby he knew his son
stalked with the very same face.
So he led out the animals—
beside the piled stones called out
to the dense woods beyond, named
his son *brother*
when a flint came flying
to his temple.

There would be only that son left—
his limbs flailing
and his face implacable as stone.

And God said, Let there be—
. . . and hesitated. Wasn't
it slightly off-key? They would get it
wrong for centuries, perhaps even
longer. A great smile
widened over the deep. God
said, Let there be a profusion
of words on the tongues
that will speak. And God knew
it would be good. It had
to be. After they mistakenly call
me *He*—oh long after,
they will finally utter *She*.
She for another few millennia
before *I* become *One*
once again.

Many of these poems first appeared
in the following journals:

*Bywords, Canadian Literature, Dis-ease,
The Fulcrum, NASA Journal, Parchment, Poet Lore,
The Tel Aviv Review, Viewpoints*;

in the following anthologies:

Six Ottawa Poets (Mosaic Press),
Without a Single Answer (Judah L. Magnes Museum),
Words We Call Home (University of British
Columbia Press);

in Hebrew translation:

Al Hamishmar, Maariv, Hadoar; and in the collection
Simple Ceremony (Hakibbutz
Hameuchad, 1990).

A few poems were included on the broadside,
Down Here (Tree, 1990), and a number were broadcast
on Radio Israel.

The author wishes to thank Multiculturalism and
Citizenship Canada for the generous assistance of a
writing grant.

This book has been published in a limited edition of 500, of which 50 copies have been signed and numbered by the author.

Seymour Mayne was born and raised in Montreal.
Editor of a number of critical texts and anthologies,
he has also translated poetry from several languages.
His collection *Name* won the J.I. Segal Prize in
English-French literature and the York Poetry
Workshop Award. His most recent volumes include
Children of Abel, and a collection of biblical poems,
Going Up. His poetry has been translated into
Spanish, French, Greek, Yiddish, Polish and Italian;
and two volumes of his work have been rendered
into Hebrew, *Vanguard of Dreams: New and
Selected Poems* and *Simple Ceremony*.